2019

Dearest Samantha,

The author, Stu—
is a personal friend of
mine! He rocks a wonderful
message!

I love you very much! ♡

xxx
xxx
Aunt Margo

:)

D1457138

ISBN 978-0-578-53078-9
Frozen Lips Publishing
P.O. Box 2082
Northbrook, IL 60065
www.TheStuShow.com

I Like to be Liked

12 THINGS TO DO
(ALL OF THE TIME)
TO BE LIKED

Written by Stuart Jacobson
Illustrated by Brelyn Giffin

HELLO

Thank you for entering the **Be Kind Be Positive and Read Conservatoire**—the place where superheroes train for success. Stu will teach you 12 things to do (all of the time) to be liked. Did you know? REPETITION is the mother of all learning! Practice, Repeat, Practice, Repeat, Practice Repeat these 12 things and you will be a superhero.

Best wishes,
Superhero Trainer Stu

POSITIVITY TRACKER

What did I do today to be positive?

DAY 1	**DAY 2**	**DAY 3**
DAY 4	**DAY 5**	**DAY 6**
DAY 7	**DAY 8**	**DAY 9**
DAY 10	**DAY 11**	**DAY 12**
DAY 13	**DAY 14**	**DAY 15**

HAPPINESS TRACKER

What did I do today to be happy?

DAY 1	**DAY 2**	**DAY 3**
DAY 4	**DAY 5**	**DAY 6**
DAY 7	**DAY 8**	**DAY 9**
DAY 10	**DAY 11**	**DAY 12**
DAY 13	**DAY 14**	**DAY 15**

I Like To Be Happy

KINDNESS TRACKER

What did I do today to be kind?

DAY 1	**DAY 2**	**DAY 3**
DAY 4	**DAY 5**	**DAY 6**
DAY 7	**DAY 8**	**DAY 9**
DAY 10	**DAY 11**	**DAY 12**
DAY 13	**DAY 14**	**DAY 15**

CONSISTENCY MATTERS!

Consistency means all of the time. To be better than average at something, you give it your all. When you are better than average, you are more likely to achieve your goals.

HELPFULNESS TRACKER

What did I do today to be helpful?

DAY 1	**DAY 2**	**DAY 3**
DAY 4	**DAY 5**	**DAY 6**
DAY 7	**DAY 8**	**DAY 9**
DAY 10	**DAY 11**	**DAY 12**
DAY 13	**DAY 14**	**DAY 15**

I Like To Be Helpful

CHEERFUL TRACKER

What did I do today to make others cheerful?

DAY 1	DAY 2	DAY 3
DAY 4	DAY 5	DAY 6
DAY 7	DAY 8	DAY 9
DAY 10	DAY 11	DAY 12
DAY 13	DAY 14	DAY 15

It Makes Others Cheerful

THOUGHTFULNESS TRACKER

What did I do today to be thoughtful?

DAY 1	**DAY 2**	**DAY 3**
DAY 4	**DAY 5**	**DAY 6**
DAY 7	**DAY 8**	**DAY 9**
DAY 10	**DAY 11**	**DAY 12**
DAY 13	**DAY 14**	**DAY 15**

I Like To Be Thoughtful

SUPERHERO TIP

To be a great musician, you practice. To be a great athlete, you practice. To be a superhero, you practice. Practice makes you GREAT!

UPBEAT TRACKER

What did I do today to be upbeat?

DAY 1	DAY 2	DAY 3
DAY 4	DAY 5	DAY 6
DAY 7	DAY 8	DAY 9
DAY 10	DAY 11	DAY 12
DAY 13	DAY 14	DAY 15

I Like To Be Upbeat

SAY NICE THINGS TRACKER

What nice things did I say today?

DAY 1	**DAY 2**	**DAY 3**
DAY 4	**DAY 5**	**DAY 6**
DAY 7	**DAY 8**	**DAY 9**
DAY 10	**DAY 11**	**DAY 12**
DAY 13	**DAY 14**	**DAY 15**

And Always Say Nice Things

USEFULNESS TRACKER

What did I do today to be useful?

DAY 1	**DAY 2**	**DAY 3**
DAY 4	**DAY 5**	**DAY 6**
DAY 7	**DAY 8**	**DAY 9**
DAY 10	**DAY 11**	**DAY 12**
DAY 13	**DAY 14**	**DAY 15**

I Like To Be Useful

SUPERHERO TIP

Make-believe superheroes wear capes and fly. They are heroes. Real superheroes wear ordinary clothes and walk. They are heroes. All superheroes have one thing in common. They are awesome, all of the time!

GROOVY TRACKER

What did I do today to be groovy?

DAY 1

DAY 2

DAY 3

DAY 4

DAY 5

DAY 6

DAY 7

DAY 8

DAY 9

DAY 10

DAY 11

DAY 12

DAY 13

DAY 14

DAY 15

SCHMOOZE TRACKER

What did I do today to schmooze?

DAY 1	**DAY 2**	**DAY 3**
DAY 4	**DAY 5**	**DAY 6**
DAY 7	**DAY 8**	**DAY 9**
DAY 10	**DAY 11**	**DAY 12**
DAY 13	**DAY 14**	**DAY 15**

Schmoozy

CHOOSY TRACKER

What did I do today to make good choices?

DAY 1	DAY 2	DAY 3
DAY 4	DAY 5	DAY 6
DAY 7	DAY 8	DAY 9
DAY 10	DAY 11	DAY 12
DAY 13	DAY 14	DAY 15

And Choosy

PETS FOR ADOPTION

THANK YOU TRACKER

Who did I say "Thank You" to today?

DAY 1

DAY 2

DAY 3

DAY 4

DAY 5

DAY 6

DAY 7

DAY 8

DAY 9

DAY 10

DAY 11

DAY 12

DAY 13

DAY 14

DAY 15

I Like To Say "Thank You"

SUPERHERO TIP

Everyone loves knowing a superhero. You too can be a
superhero by following these 12 things all of the time.

MOST LIKELY TO SUCCEED

I Like To Be Positive

I Like To Be Happy

THIS IS NOT THE END...
IT IS ONLY THE BEGINNING!

BE KIND
BE POSITIVE
AND READ

for a safer and friendlier world!

Help Stu spread this very important message by booking him at your school, library or festival.
Contact: stuart@frozenlips.com.

12 THINGS TO DO
(ALL OF THE TIME)
TO BE LIKED

ABOUT THE AUTHOR

America's #1 Superhero Instructor Stuart Jacobson travels throughout America performing his motivational children's show, *Be Kind Be Positive and Read*, at schools, libraries and festivals. Stu teaches three simple rules for becoming a successful superhero: Be Kind Be Positive and Read.

Stu is a speaker, author, musician, songwriter and sociologist. He has dedicated his life to researching, investigating and studying human charm, charisma, appeal and success. His purpose has been clear. Why are some people LIKED more than others? Stuart has taken his findings and studied them, scrutinized them, analyzed them, dissected them, questioned them and debated them. He found that successful social interaction is NOT complicated. In fact, it is quite simple. Stuart loves to share his findings with both young and old audiences alike.

ABOUT THE ILLUSTRATOR

Brelyn Giffin lives in Los Angeles as a freelance illustrator. She is a self-taught artist who enjoys creating character concepts and designs, and draws her inspiration from a mixture of Western and Japanese graphic novels. When she's not working, she spends her time reading an unhealthy amount of Batman comics, playing video games, and snuggling with her dog, Toast.

CPSIA information can be obtained
at www.ICGtesting.com
Printed in the USA
LVHW070511170719
624364LV00019B/229/P